I've Got to MOVE!

12 Active Songs for Elementary Music Classes
by Tim Brophy

- ☺ Movement or dances for all songs
- ☺ CD included with full performance and accompaniment tracks
- ☺ Complete lesson plans
- ☺ Assessment strategies
- ☺ Correlated to the National Standards for Music Education

Kid-Tested!

 CD INCLUDED

Editor: Gayle Giese
Recording Producer: Teena Chinn
Art Design: Nancy Rehm

WARNER BROS. PUBLICATIONS
Warner Music Group
An AOL Time Warner Company
USA: 15800 NW 48th Avenue, Miami, FL 33014

WARNER/CHAPPELL MUSIC
CANADA: 15800 N.W. 48th AVENUE
MIAMI, FLORIDA 33014
SCANDINAVIA: P.O. BOX 533, VENDEVAGEN 85 B
S-182 15, DANDERYD, SWEDEN
AUSTRALIA: P.O. BOX 353
3 TALAVERA ROAD, NORTH RYDE N.S.W. 2113
ASIA: THE PENINSULA OFFICE TOWER, 12th FLOOR
18 MIDDLE ROAD
TSIM SHA TSUI, KOWLOON, HONG KONG

NUOVA CARISCH
ITALY: VIA CAMPANIA, 12
20098 S. GIULIANO MILANESE (MI)
ZONA INDUSTRIALE SESTO ULTERIANO
SPAIN: MAGALLANES, 25
28015 MADRID
FRANCE: CARISCH MUSICOM,
25, RUE D'HAUTEVILLE, 75010 PARIS

INTERNATIONAL MUSIC PUBLICATIONS LIMITED
ENGLAND: GRIFFIN HOUSE,
161 HAMMERSMITH ROAD, LONDON W6 8BS
GERMANY: MARSTALLSTR. 8, D-80539 MUNCHEN
DENMARK: DANMUSIK, VOGNMAGERGADE 7
DK 1120 KOBENHAVNK

MW01097946

Dedicated to my dear wife, Emmie

Introduction

I've Got to Move! is a collection of 12 songs that are engaging and fun! Written for elementary music classes, they combine activity with singing in a way that children enjoy. The lessons include activities that range from doing simple hand movements to creating original dances. These songs have all been put to the test in my own music classroom, and each has become a favorite of my students.

To assist you in implementing these songs, each has been correlated with the appropriate National Standard(s), and a specific process for teaching the song and the movement has been included. Also, when possible, notes and tips are included that will help expedite the teaching and learning of the songs. For those of you who are guitarists, the guitar chords are provided; an accompaniment CD is also included. The enclosed CD includes both vocal (full performance) and instrumental (accompaniment) tracks for the songs.

An assessment task has been designed for each song, and the framework for each assessment task has been included. The assessment frameworks include the type of task designed, the assessable component, assessment response mode, assessment tool, the materials required to complete the assessment, and the scoring guide for the task.

The National Standards correlations, teaching processes, notes and tips, and assessments and their frameworks help to make these songs seamless additions to your curriculum. The accompaniment CD makes the songs easy to introduce to your classes. I hope these songs are as enjoyable for your students as they have been for mine!

Timothy S. Brophy, Ph.D.
University of Florida

Timothy S. Brophy

Timothy S. Brophy teaches undergraduate and graduate music education courses at the University of Florida in Gainesville and holds a bachelor's degree in music education from the University of Cincinnati College–Conservatory of Music, a master of music degree with a concentration in Orff Schulwerk from the University of Memphis, and a Ph.D. in music education from the University of Kentucky. As an elementary music teacher, Dr. Brophy was awarded an Ashland Teacher Achievement Award (1996) and a Memphis Rotary Club Rotary Award for Teacher Excellence (1999) and was the first elementary music teacher to be honored at the Disney American Teacher Awards in Los Angeles in 1998. An active music education writer and clinician, Dr. Brophy's articles have appeared in the *Music Educator's Journal, Teaching Music,* the *Orff Echo, Tennessee Musician,* and *Tennessee Teacher.* He is author of the books *Assessing the Developing Child Musician: A Guide for General Music Teachers* (2000, GIA Publications) and *I've Got to Move!* (2002, Warner Bros. Publications). Dr. Brophy's research interests include musical creativity (improvisation), musical development, and assessment. He continues to present his research at numerous conferences both in the United States and abroad, and his research has been published in *Contributions to Music Education,* the *Southeastern Journal of Music Education,* and *The Canadian Music Educator.* He is currently serving as editor of the journal *Research Perspectives in Music Education* and is a member of the editorial boards of *The Music Educators Journal,* the *Orff Echo,* and *Research and Issues in Music Education.* He has been chair of the Research Advisory Review Panel of the American Orff-Schulwerk Association (AOSA) and is the national conference co-chair for the AOSA 2003 National Conference and chair of the Florida Music Assessment Task Force.

Contents

Recommended Grade Levels: K–1

National Content Standard:
1—Singing, alone and with others, a varied repertoire of music

I Hear a Bird in a Tree

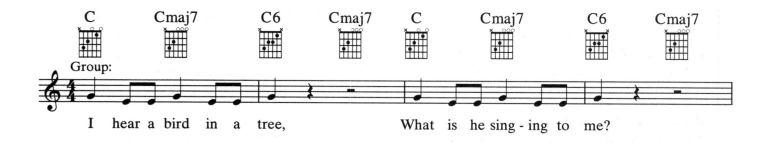

Group:

I hear a bird in a tree, What is he sing-ing to me?

Solo, unaccompanied:

Cuc - koo Cuc - cuc - koo, Cuc - koo, Cuc - cuc - koo.

This song is recorded three times, with a 5-second pause between each repetition.

I Hear a Bird in a Tree

☺ Teaching Process:

1. Gather the children in a circle, and let them know you are going to teach them a special song that is also a game.

2. Sing this song for the children, and ask them to listen carefully because when the song is finished, you will ask them to describe the story the song tells. During the discussion of the story, sing it again several times to reinforce the children's aural memory of the melody and words. *Tip: By asking the children to recall the story of the song, you are indirectly encouraging them to remember the words.*

3. If your students have studied solfège and know the pitches *sol* and *mi,* ask the boys and girls to tell you what pitches they are singing. (This is aural identification of *sol* and *mi.*)

4. Once they know the song, describe that it is to be sung in two sections—one section by the group (the question, "What is s/he singing to me?") and one by the "bird" (the cuckoo). Explain that this time they will practice singing only the bird's part—the "cuckoo"—and you will sing the question. Once you try this and they understand, switch the parts, allowing them to sing the questions while you sing the cuckoo.

5. Teach the game (instructions below). If possible, play the game until all of the children have had a turn to be the bird.

☺ Game: I Hear a Bird in a Tree

All of the children but one scatter about the room, close their eyes, and shape their bodies into "trees," creating a "forest." The remaining child becomes a "bird." While the "trees" sing the group section of the song, the "bird" silently "flies" around the room and by the end of the group section has landed behind one of the "trees." The "bird" becomes a soloist and sings the "cuckoo" phrases, and the "tree" children must then silently indicate they know where the "bird"/soloist is by listening and pointing toward the "bird"/soloist. The "trees" then open their eyes to see if they were correct. When all of the "trees" have found the "bird," the game resumes with the "tree" by whom the "bird" landed becoming the new "bird." The former "bird" then sits on the floor as a "bush" (this helps the teacher keep track of who has had a turn). The "bushes" still play the game from a sitting position, and the new "bird" never lands on a "bush." *Tip: When demonstrating all group/solo games, it is best for you to demonstrate the solo part first for the children. For this game, you should demonstrate the role of the bird as the children in the "forest" leave their eyes open to watch what the bird does.*

☺ Assessment: *Technical Musical Skill Development: Vocal Pitch Accuracy*

What: Do the children demonstrate vocal pitch accuracy on *sol* and *mi* during their solo performance of the "cuckoo" phrases?

How:

1. Inform the children that you will be listening to their performance of the "cuckoo" phrases when they are the bird to check for how well they are matching the *sol* and *mi* pitches they are singing. *Note: The children should know that the pitches in the song are all on sol-mi.* Explain that you will be marking their performance as follows: They will receive a "+" (plus) if they are accurate on *sol* and *mi*; a "|" (half plus) if they are not accurate; and a "~" if their pitches waver or "move around." To establish a sense of security in the children, you may want to first do this exercise just by telling them that you will be observing (without marking/grading) their "cuckoo" performances and coaching them on ways to improve their singing. *Tip: The fixed pitches you use should be pitches that your school district curriculum states should be acquired or experienced in grades K–1—most often where do = middle c, d, or f.*

2. As the children play the game, listen to their solos and determine the accuracy of their pitches. Mark your data collection instrument—grade book, seating chart, etc.—according to your observations. *Tip: Be careful not to change a child's marking because of incorrect lyrics—you are judging only pitch accuracy.*

☺ Assessment Framework:

Type: Formative, Structured Experience
Assessable Component: Technical Musical Skill Achievement: Vocal Pitch Accuracy
Assessment Response Mode: Performance
Tool: Observation
Materials: Data collection instrument, pen or pencil for marking
Scoring Guide: Multilevel, single criterion
Criterion: The student sings *sol* and *mi* on pitch
Levels of Achievement: + = demonstrated; | = not demonstrated; ~ = pitch wavers

Full Track 3 • Accompaniment Track 4

Recommended Grade Levels: K–1

National Content Standard:
1—Singing, alone and with others, a varied repertoire of music

The Giant Song

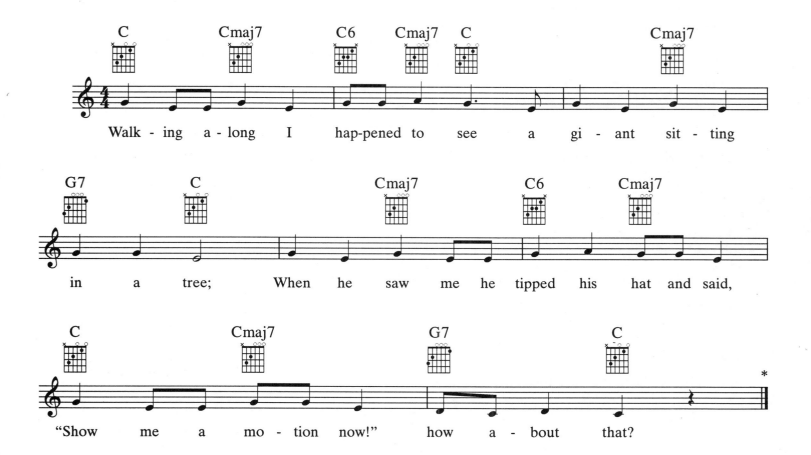

*This song is recorded three times and followed each time
by 16 measures of "walking," "rock," or "plodding" music.*

The Giant Song

⊚ Teaching Process:

1. Sing this song for the children, and ask them to listen carefully because when the song is finished, you will ask them to describe the story the song tells. During the discussion of the story, sing it again several times so that the children have plenty of opportunity to hear the melody and words. *Tip: By asking the children to recall the story of the song, you are indirectly encouraging them to remember the words.*

2. Ask the children to join you in singing the song, and do this a few times until you feel that they know the song well enough to add the movements, as follows:

   Walking   along   I   happened   to   see
   Movement: walking happily in place, or around the room

   A   giant   sitting   in   a   tree
   Movement: pointing upward to an imaginary tree, disbelieving

   When   he   saw   me   he   tipped   his   hat   and   said
   Movement: point to self,   pretend to "tip your hat"

   Show   me   a   motion!   How   about   that?
   Movement: pointing downward in a "demanding" way, then hands up in a "what's up?" gesture

3. Once the children know the movement and the song, permit them to move about the room, singing and dramatizing the song once or twice more.

4. Then, instruct the children that you will play some music for them to show off their movement for the "Giant." *Tip: This music can be improvised at the piano, or you may use the CD prerecorded music for this, and should be 16 measures long. During this music, the children should create a dance for the "giant."*

5. At this time the children are ready to sing the song, and then add their dance. It is important to tell them that their dance should be different each time they perform the song.

◎ Assessment: *Enabling Competency: Kinesthetic Response to Music*

What: Are the children creating a dance in response to the music?

How:

1. Inform the children that you will be observing them during their dance to see if they are able to make up a dance to the music you play. If you are improvising music for this assessment, be sure to change your improvised music at least three times during the 16 measures of the dance in order to check for the changes in the children's movement responses. *Note: The CD recorded music does this.* Explain that you will be marking their performance as follows: They will receive a "+" (plus) if their dance changes with the music, a "|" (half plus) if their dance does not change with the music, and a "0" if they are not dancing at all. To establish a sense of security in the children, you may want to first do this exercise just by telling them that you will be observing (without marking/grading) their dancing and coaching them on ways to improve their movements to the music.

2. As the children create their dances, observe them closely for whether or not they change their movements in response to the music. Mark your data collection instrument—grade book, seating chart, and so on—according to your observations.

◎ Assessment Framework:

Type: Formative, Structured Experience
Assessable Component: Enabling Competency: Kinesthetic Response to Music
Assessment Response Mode: Performance
Tool: Observation
Materials: Data collection instrument, pen or pencil for marking
Scoring Guide: Multilevel, single criterion
Criterion: The student creates a dance in response to the music
Levels of Achievement: + = demonstrated; | = not demonstrated; 0 = no movement response

Recommended Grade Levels: 2–3

National Content Standards:
1—Singing, alone and with others, a varied repertoire of music
6—Listening to and analyzing music (form—AB)

Hello and Howdy

This song is recorded three times, up a half-step each time (ABABAB).

Hello and Howdy

⊘ Teaching Process:

1. Sing the song for the children, and add the hand movements as follows:

   Hello and   howdy to   my   friends
   Movement: *wave one or both hands at those around you*

   Hello to   the   whole world end   to   end;
   Movement: *wave hands…then point out the "ends" with both hands wide, gesturing a "bookend" with each hand on each word "end," one hand at a time*

   Hello and   howdy to my friends   on
   Movement: *same as first phrase*

   This   new   day!
   Movement: *roll arms on "this new" and open them on "day!"*

2. Teach the song by rote, one phrase and movement at a time, or by having the children sing a little more each time you perform this.

3. Teach the **B** section, one phrase at a time. *Tip: Identify the phrases with numbers—phrase 1, phrase 2, and so on. Then, when it is time to practice the phrases consecutively, refer to phrase 1 followed by 2 as "phrase 12," and phrase 1 followed by 2 and then 3 as "phrase 123," and phrase 1 followed by 2 and then 3 and then 4 as "phrase 1,234." This keeps the sequence of phrases foremost in the children's minds in an amusing and engaging way. This procedure is also used in "Welcome Song."*

4. When the class knows the **B** section, add the **A** section and perform once.

5. Ask the children to perform the song as they move around the room while singing it, placing the steady half-note ($\downarrow$) macrobeat in their feet. *Note: A partner is not necessary for the **B** section; however, it can be done facing a partner if desired.*

6. Lead the children to discover the form of the song—**AB**.

⊚ Assessment: *Enabling Competency: Steady Beat*

What: Do the children demonstrate the steady beat during the performance of the song?

How:

1. Inform the children that you will be observing their performance of the song and dance to check for their ability to demonstrate the steady beat in a consistent manner. Explain that you will be marking their performance as follows: They will receive a "+" (plus) if they are demonstrating the beat consistently and a "|" (half plus) if they are not. To establish a sense of security in the children, you may want to first do this exercise just by telling them that you will be observing (without marking/grading) them and coaching them on demonstrating a steady beat.

2. As the children step to the half-note macrobeat, observe them closely for their demonstration of the steady beat. Mark your data collection instrument—grade book, seating chart, and so on—according to your observations.

⊚ Assessment Framework:

Type: Formative, Structured Experience
Assessable Component: Enabling Competency: Steady Beat
Assessment Response Mode: Performance
Tool: Observation
Materials: Data collection instrument, pen or pencil for marking
Scoring Guide: Bilevel, single criterion
Criterion: The student demonstrates the steady beat
Levels of Achievement: + = demonstrated; | = not demonstrated

Recommended Grade Level: 3

National Content Standards:
1—Singing, alone and with others, a varied repertoire of music
6—Listening to and analyzing music (form—**AB**)

I Feel the Joy!

A Section

With a "swing"

I feel the joy when I sing a song,— I feel the joy as I move a - long,— I feel the joy when I sing and play,— and I know it's going to be a great— new day!

(To B Section)

B Section Dance

Snap
Clap
Patsch
Stamp

*(Repeat A and B Sections as desired; Fine last time)**

Snap
Clap
Patsch
Stamp

This song is recorded three times, down a half-step the second time (ABABAB).

I Feel the Joy!

🌀 Teaching Process:

1. Form a circle, and begin step-snapping to the quarter-note beat (♩), like this:

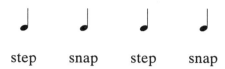

     step   snap   step   snap

2. Ask the children to join you. Once they have joined in the step-snap, sing the song for them. *Tip: It is helpful to have the words of the song and the poem on a poster or chart for the children to read.*
3. Teach the song by rote, by phrases, or by having the children start singing along with you as soon as they know the song.
4. When they can sing the song independently (without you singing along), ask them to sing the song while moving around the room with the steady beat in their feet. Once they are comfortable with this, invite them to dramatize the words to the song as they walk around the room, creating their own "dance" as they sing.
5. The **B** section of this song is a body-percussion sequence that uses stamping, patschen (patting the lap), clapping, and snapping. Teach the **B** section by having the children echo you one phrase at a time. As you introduce the phrases to the **B** section and the children copy them, be sure to make the sequence cumulative, using the technique described in "Welcome Song."
6. Once the **B** section is learned, add this to the song and perform the song several times.
7. Lead the children to discover the form of the song—**AB**.

🌀 Assessment: *Enabling Competency: Steady Beat and Creative Movement: Appropriateness of Movement*

What: Do the children demonstrate the steady beat and appropriate movement response during the performance of the song?

How:

1. Inform the children that you will be observing their performance of the song and dance to check for their ability to demonstrate the steady beat in a consistent manner and to create appropriate movement to the words of the song. Explain that you will be marking their performance as follows: They will receive a "+" (plus) if they are demonstrating the beat consistently and a "|" (half plus) if they are not and that they will receive a "+" (plus) if their movements are appropriate, a "|" (half plus) if the movements are not appropriate, and a "0" if they are not creating any movements at all. *Tip: It is recommended that the children have a clear idea of what "appropriate movements" are for this song so they know how to earn a "+"—the best way to do this is to ask the children to demonstrate movements that are both appropriate and inappropriate. Once they make a clear distinction between the two types of movements, explain that now they have shown you that they know the difference, so there is no reason for any of them to "accidentally" move in an inappropriate manner.*

2. As the children create movements and step to the beat, observe them closely for their demonstration of the steady beat and the appropriateness of their created movements. Mark your data collection instrument—grade book, seating chart, and so on—according to your observations.

◎ Assessment Framework:

Type: Formative, Structured Experience
Assessable Component: Enabling Competency: Steady Beat; Creative Movement: Appropriateness of Movement
Assessment Response Mode: Performance
Tool: Observation
Materials: Data collection instrument, pen or pencil for marking
Scoring Guide: Multilevel, single criterion
Criterion: The student demonstrates the steady beat
Levels of Achievement: + = demonstrated; | = not demonstrated; 0 = no movement response

Full Track 9

Accompaniment Track 10

Recommended Grade Level: 3

National Content Standards:
1—Singing, alone and with others, a varied repertoire of music
6—Listening to and analyzing music (form—AB)

Looking Good, Feeling Great!

A Section

With confidence and excitement

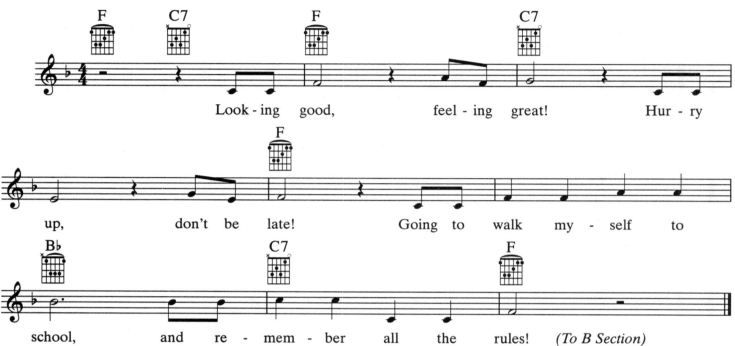

Look-ing good,   feel-ing great!   Hur-ry
up,   don't be late!   Going to walk my-self to
school,   and re-mem-ber all the rules!   *(To B Section)*

B Section Poem

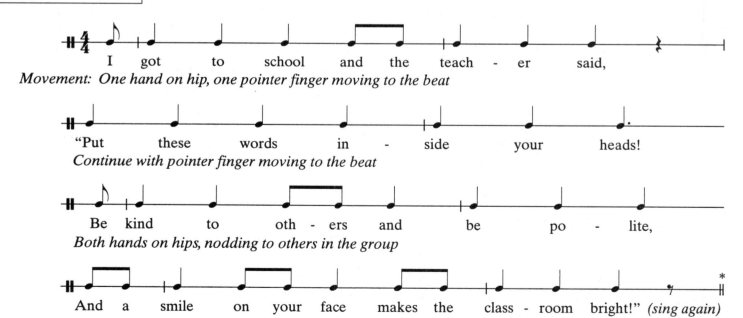

I got   to   school   and   the   teach-er   said,
Movement: One hand on hip, one pointer finger moving to the beat

"Put   these   words   in-side   your   heads!
Continue with pointer finger moving to the beat

Be   kind   to   oth-ers   and   be   po-lite,
Both hands on hips, nodding to others in the group

And   a   smile   on   your   face   makes   the   class-room   bright!"   *(sing again)*

*With both hands in a criss-cross motion, make a "smile" by drawing it underneath the lips on
the chin on the word "smile," then "explode" the hands outward in a circle on "classroom bright!"*

This song is recorded three times (ABABAB).

Looking Good, Feeling Great!

◎ Teaching Process:

1. Form a circle, and begin snapping or lightly stepping the steady beat. Sing the song for the children. Teach the song by rote, either by having the children join the singing when they know the song or by teaching it one phrase at a time. Move the steady beat to different body percussion as you teach the song—for instance, snapping, patting the lap, stepping in place, clapping lightly.

2. Ask the class what movements might be appropriate for such a song—gesturing to point out how "good" they look and feel, movements indicating "hurry up" and "don't be late," and so on—and lead them in trying out a few.

3. Next, lead the class to create a set of movements appropriate for each phrase, and have the class perform these original movements while singing the song.

4. Remaining in the circle, perform the **B** section poem and movements for the class.

5. Perform the song, followed by the poem. When the children are familiar with the form, invite them to put the beat in their feet, leave their spot in the circle, and move around the room as they sing the song, stopping when the poem begins so that it is performed in place.

6. Lead the children to discover the form of the song—**AB**.

◎ Assessment: *Enabling Competencies: Steady Beat*

What: Do the children demonstrate the steady beat during the performance of the song?

How:

1. Inform the children that you will be observing their performance of the song and dance to check for their ability to demonstrate the steady beat in a consistent manner. Explain that you will be marking their performance as follows: They will receive a "+" (plus) if they are demonstrating the beat consistently and a "|" (half plus) if they are not. To establish a sense of security in the children, you may want to first do this exercise just by telling them that you will be observing (without marking/grading) their ability to move to a steady beat and coaching them.

2. As the children step to the beat, observe them closely for their demonstration of the steady beat. Mark your data collection instrument—grade book, seating chart, and so on—according to your observations.

◎ Assessment Framework:

Type: Formative, Structured Experience
Assessable Component: Enabling Competency: Steady Beat
Assessment Response Mode: Performance
Tool: Observation
Materials: Data collection instrument, pen or pencil for marking
Scoring Guide: Bilevel, single criterion
Criterion: The student demonstrates the steady beat
Levels of Achievement: + = demonstrated; | = not demonstrated

Full
Track
11

Accompaniment
Track
12

Recommended Grade Level: 4

National Content Standards:
1—Singing, alone and with others, a varied repertoire of music
6—Listening to and analyzing music (form—**ABA**)

Find a Friend

A Section

Let's take a walk and find a friend,___
Final Verse: Let's take a walk and find our seats,___

find a friend,_ find a friend._ Let's take a walk and
find our seats,_ find our seats._ Let's take a walk and

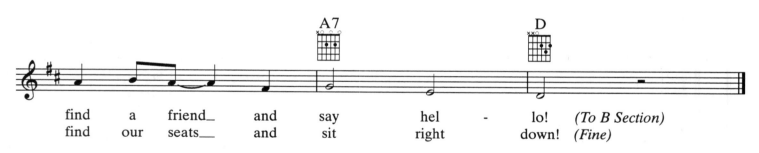

find a friend_ and say hel - lo! *(To B Section)*
find our seats_ and sit right down! *(Fine)*

B Section Poem and Body Percussion

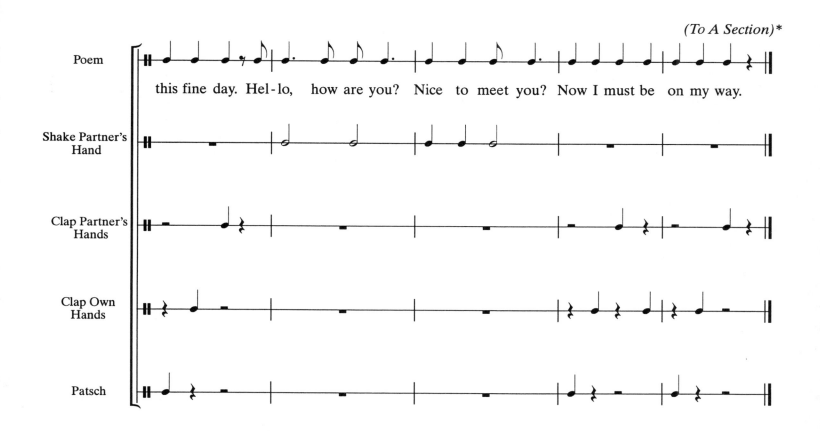

This song is recorded in ABABA form.

Find a Friend

☺ Teaching Process:

1. Form a circle, and begin step-snapping to the quarter-note beat (♩), like this:

   step snap step snap

2. Ask the children to join you. Once they have joined in the step-snap, sing the song for them. *Tip: It is helpful to have the words of the song and the poem on a poster or chart for the children to read.*

3. Teach the song by rote, by phrases, or by having the children start singing as soon as they know the song.

4. When they know the song, invite the students to move with the step-snap, and when they get to the "say hello" words in the song, they should find themselves next to someone in the class who is near them. *Tip: It's important to remind the class that everyone is a friend in the music room, and therefore it does not matter who they are next to at the end of the song.*

5. Ask the class to face you. Then teach the poem and the movements of the **B** section, having the children practice the movements "in the air" without a partner.

6. Once they can recite the entire poem and demonstrate the movements without a partner, ask a child to come to the front of the class to be your partner. Demonstrate the **B** section poem with your child partner.

7. Have the children turn to face the person by whom they are standing (the same classmate they were next to at the end of the song), and lead them in the speaking of the poem and movement with that partner.

8. Once they have learned the **B** section and demonstrated this with a partner, instruct them that they will now step-snap and sing the song again, moving around the room until the end of the song, when they will be next to a different classmate. They will then go right into the **B** section, speaking the poem and movement with that partner.

9. Sing the song several times, finding new partners for the **B** section each time. For the final verse, change the words to:
   Let's take a walk and find our seats, find our seats, find our seats,
   Let's take a walk and find our seats and sit right down! (no **B** section for the last verse).

10. Lead the children to discover the form of the song—**ABA**.

◎ Assessment: *Enabling Competency: Steady Beat*

What: Do the children demonstrate the steady beat during the performance of the song?

How:

1. Inform the children that you will be observing their performance of the song/poem to check for their ability to demonstrate the steady beat in a consistent manner. Explain that you will be marking their performance as follows: They will receive a "+" (plus) if they are demonstrating the beat consistently and a "|" (half plus) if they are not. To establish a sense of security in the children, you may want to first do this exercise just by telling them that you will be observing (without marking/grading) their performances and helping them with ways to demonstrate the steady beat.

2. As the children perform the step-snap movement in the **A** section, observe them closely for their demonstration of the steady beat. Mark your data collection instrument—grade book, seating chart, and so on—according to your observations.

◎ Assessment Framework:

Type: Formative, Structured Experience
Assessable Component: Enabling Competency: Steady Beat
Assessment Response Mode: Performance
Tool: Observation
Materials: Data collection instrument, pen or pencil for marking
Scoring Guide: Bilevel, single criterion
Criterion: The student demonstrates the steady beat
Levels of Achievement: + = demonstrated; | = not demonstrated

Full Track 13

Accompaniment Track 14

Recommended Grade Level: 4

National Content Standards:
1—Singing, alone and with others, a varied repertoire of music
6—Listening to and analyzing music (form—**AB**)

I've Got to Move!

A Section

I've got to move! I've got to shake! I've got to

step, step, step, but not in place! I'd like to shake your hand____ and

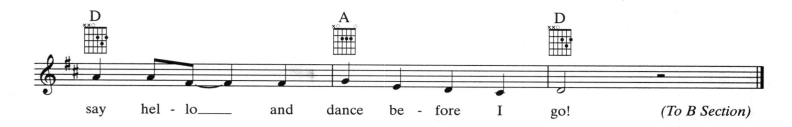

say hel - lo____ and dance be - fore I go! *(To B Section)*

B Section Dance

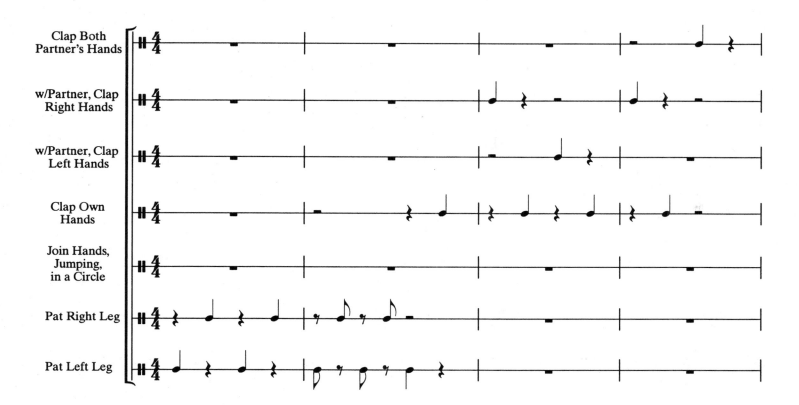

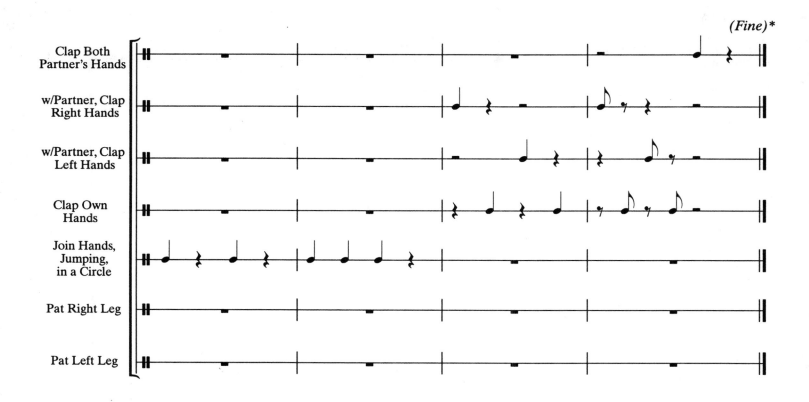

*This song is recorded three times, up a half-step each time (ABABAB).

I've Got to Move!

◎ Teaching Process:

1. Form a circle, and begin step-snapping to the quarter-note beat (♩), like this:

       step   snap   step   snap

2. Ask the children to join you. Once they have joined in the step-snap, sing the song for them. *Tip: It is helpful to have the words of the song and the poem on a poster or chart for the children to read.*

3. Teach the song by rote, by phrases, or by having the children start singing as soon as they know the song.

4. Invite the children to dramatize the words as they sing in place. *Tip: Their movements should be spontaneous and fit the words; these should not be prescribed.*

5. Once the children can sing the song and dramatize the words, ask them to move about the room to the step of the step-snap they used when they learned the words of the song. *Tip: They will step to the half-note macrobeat, ♩. At the end of the song, they should be next to a classmate.*

6. Have the children face you (they will no longer be in a circle). Teach the B section one phrase at a time, demonstrating the movements without a partner. The children should also practice these movements "in the air" without a partner.

7. Ask for a child volunteer to be your partner as you demonstrate the movement as it is done with a partner. *Tip: Be sure to demonstrate gentle clapping of the partner's hands, especially in phrase 4, because when children are attempting physically challenging body percussion, they sometimes can clap too hard, potentially hurting their partner. Be sure to hold both of the partner's hands for phrase 3, and you can help the children learn this movement by adding the following words:*

    Jump,   jump,   turn a - round.

Once the children know this phrase, they can perform it "thinking" the words and not saying them aloud.

8. After the children observe you and the child volunteer, have them turn to face the classmate next to them. Lead them in the **B** section with their own partners.

9. Once they know the **B** section, add the song and perform it three or four times, finding new partners each time.

⊚ Assessment: *Creative Movement: Appropriateness of Movement*

What: Are the children creating appropriate movement in response to the words of the song?

How:

1. Inform the children that you will be observing their created movements as they sing the song to check for their ability to create movements that are appropriate for the words. Explain that you will be marking their performance as follows: They will receive a "+" (plus) if their movements are appropriate, a "|" (half plus) if the movements are not appropriate, and a "0" if they are not creating any movements at all. *Tip: It is recommended that the children have a clear idea of what "appropriate movements" are—the best way to do this is to ask the children to demonstrate movements that are both appropriate and inappropriate. Once they make a clear distinction between the two types of movements, explain that now they have shown you that they know the difference, so there is no reason for any of them to "accidentally" move in an inappropriate manner.*

2. As the children sing the song, observe them closely for the appropriateness of their movements. Mark your data collection instrument—grade book, seating chart, and so on—according to your observations.

⊚ Assessment Framework:

Type: Formative, Structured Experience
Assessable Component: Creative Movement: Appropriateness of Movement
Assessment Response Mode: Performance
Tool: Observation
Materials: Data collection instrument, pen or pencil for marking
Scoring Guide: Multilevel, single criterion
Criterion: The student creates appropriate movement in response to the words of the song
Levels of Achievement: + = demonstrated; | = not demonstrated; 0 = no movement response

Full Track 15

Accompaniment Track 16

Recommended Grade Levels: 4–5

National Content Standards:
1—Singing, alone and with others, a varied repertoire of music
6—Listening to and analyzing music (form—**AB**)

Welcome Song

A Section

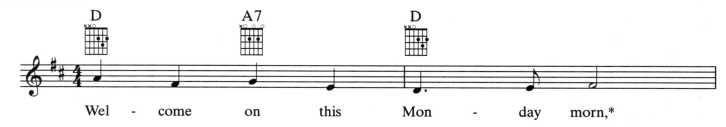

Wel - come on this Mon - day morn,*

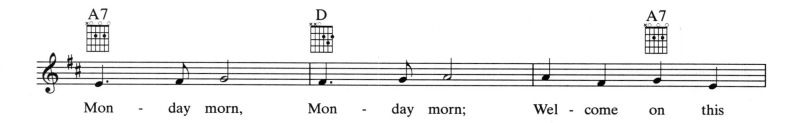

Mon - day morn, Mon - day morn; Wel - come on this

Mon - day morn, let's sing and dance to - geth - er. *(To B Section)*

*This can be changed to any day of the week, or the words
"Monday morn" can be replaced with "music class" if desired.*

B Section Dance

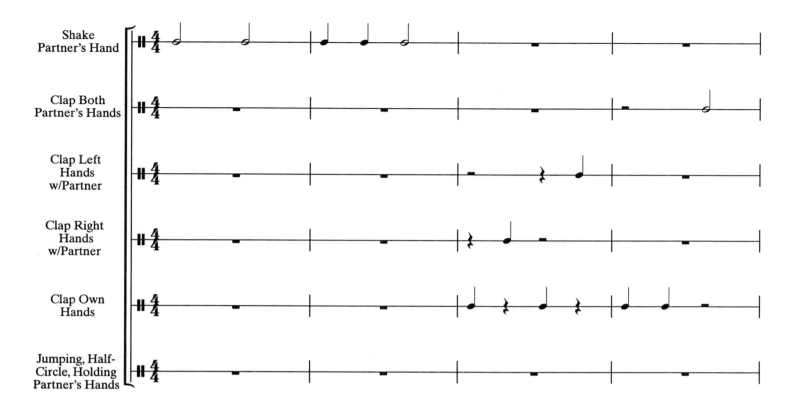

(Perform A and B Sections 3-4 times; Fine last time)**

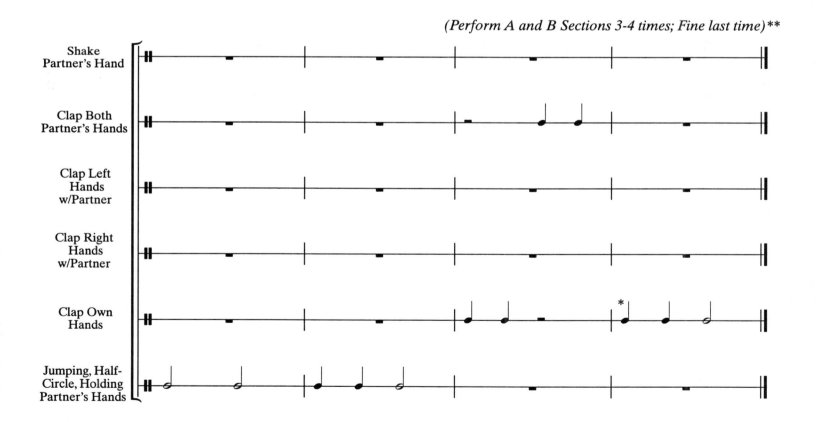

*During these three claps, jump on each rhythmic value, turning around one half-circle to face your new partner, who was behind you.

**This song is recorded three times, up a half-step each time (ABABAB).

Welcome Song

Teaching Process:

1. Form a circle, and begin snapping or lightly stepping the steady beat. Sing the song for the children. Teach the song by rote, either by having the children join the singing when they know the song or by teaching it one phrase at a time. Move the steady beat to different body percussion as you teach the song—for instance, snapping, patting the lap, stepping in place, clapping lightly.

2. Ask the class what movements might be appropriate for such a song—waving, nodding to those around you, and so on—and lead them in trying out a few. Next, ask them to create their own set of "greeting and welcoming" movements as they sing the song once again.

3. Have the children count off by two's around the circle—1, 2, 1, 2, and so on, until each child has a number. Ask the 1's to raise their hands; ask the 2's to turn toward the "1" on their right. This will be their partner for the **B** section. Once they know who their partner is, they should turn again and face you.

4. Teach the **B** section one phrase at a time, as follows: First, demonstrate the phrase "in the air" without a partner; next, have the children echo your movement without a partner; then, have them try the movement with their partner. As you teach each phrase of the dance (there are four total), review each learned set of phrases consecutively before moving on to teaching a new one. *Tip: Children enjoy the playful use of words, so identify the phrases in the dance by using phrase numbers—phrase 1, phrase 2, and so on—and when it is time to practice the phrases consecutively, refer to phrase 1 followed by 2 as "phrase 12," phrase 1 followed by 2 followed by 3 as "phrase 123," and then the entire dance becomes "phrase 1,234." This keeps the sequence of phrases foremost in the children's minds in an amusing and engaging way.*

5. Once the **B** section is learned and can be demonstrated, add the **A** section song. Perform the song and dance three or four times; each time, the children will have new partners for the dance.

6. Lead the children to discover the form of the song—**AB**.

Assessment: *Enabling Competency: Kinesthetic Response to Music*

What: Do the children demonstrate appropriate movements during the performance of the song?

How:

1. Inform the children that you will be observing their performance of the song to check for their ability to demonstrate appropriate movements. Explain that you will be marking their performance as follows: They will receive a "+" (plus) if they are demonstrating appropriate movements, a "|" (half plus) if they are not, and a "0" if they are not moving at all. *Tip: It is recommended that the children have a clear idea of what "appropriate movements" are—the best way to do this is to ask the children to demonstrate movements that are both appropriate and inappropriate. Once they make a clear distinction between the two types of movements, explain that now they have shown you that they know the difference, so there is no reason for any of them to "accidentally" move in an inappropriate manner.*
2. As the children create and perform their movement in the **A** section, observe them closely for the appropriateness of the movement and their movement response. Mark your data collection instrument—grade book, seating chart, and so on—according to your observations.

Assessment Framework:

Type: Formative, Structured Experience
Assessable Component: Enabling Competency: Kinesthetic Response to Music
Assessment Response Mode: Performance
Tool: Observation
Materials: Data collection instrument, pen or pencil for marking
Scoring Guide: Multilevel, single criterion
Criterion: The student demonstrates appropriate movements during the performance of the song
Levels of Achievement: + = demonstrated; | = not demonstrated; 0 = no movement response

Recommended Grade Levels: 4–5

National Content Standard:
1—Singing, alone and with others, a varied repertoire of music

It's a Brand New Day

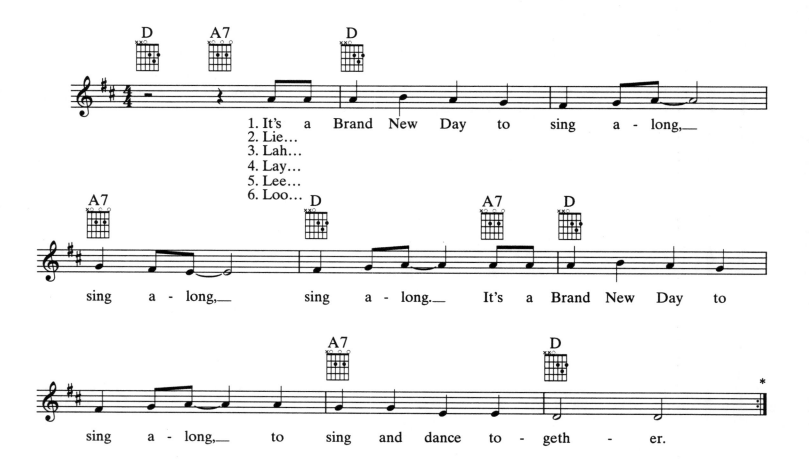

1. It's a Brand New Day to sing a-long,__
2. Lie...
3. Lah...
4. Lay...
5. Lee...
6. Loo...

sing a-long,__ sing a-long.__ It's a Brand New Day to

sing a-long,__ to sing and dance to-geth-er.

This song is recorded six times, up a half-step each time, with an 8-measure interlude for movement inserted between repeats. This makes a great vocal warmup!

It's a Brand New Day

☺ Teaching Process:

1. Teach the song by rote, in phrases, or by having the children listen to you sing it several times and asking them to join in the song as they learn it. Have the children step the half-note macrobeat (♩) as you teach the song.

2. This song makes a good active vocal warm-up for either the music class or the choir when repeated verses are sung using only vowels preceded by a consonant of your choice—such as *lie, lah, lay, lee,* or *loo. Tip: If using this as a warm-up, you should accompany the singing at the piano and move the key up and/or down a half step each time the song repeats.* A suggested movement for this is as follows:

	♩	♩	♩	♩	♩	♩	♩	♩
To the right:	RF	LF	RF	LF	RF	LF	RF	LF
	step	*touch*	*step*	*touch*	*step*	*touch*	*step*	*touch toe only*

	♩	♩	♩	♩	♩	♩	♩	♩
To the left:	LF	RF	LF	RF	LF	RF	LF	RF
	step	*touch*	*step*	*touch*	*step*	*touch*	*step*	*touch*

Invite the children to create movement variations.

☺ Assessment: *Enabling Competency: Steady Beat*

What: Do the children demonstrate the steady beat during the performance of the song?

How:

1. Inform the children that you will be observing their performance of the song/poem to check for their ability to demonstrate the steady beat in a consistent manner. Explain that you will be marking their performance as follows: They will receive a "+" (plus) if they are demonstrating the beat consistently and a "|" (half plus) if they are not. To establish a sense of security in the children, you may want to first do this exercise just by telling them that you will be observing (without marking/grading) their performances and helping them with ways to demonstrate the steady beat.

2. As the children step to the half-note macrobeat, observe them closely for their demonstration of the steady beat. Mark your data collection instrument—grade book, seating chart, and so on—according to your observations.

ⓔ Assessment Framework:

Type: Formative, Structured Experience
Assessable Component: Enabling Competency: Steady Beat
Assessment Response Mode: Performance
Tool: Observation
Materials: Data collection instrument, pen or pencil for marking
Scoring Guide: Bilevel, single criterion
Criterion: The student demonstrates the steady beat
Levels of Achievement: + = demonstrated; | = not demonstrated

Full Track 19 · Accompaniment Track 20

Everybody Come, Gather Around
(Four-part Canon with Circle Dance)

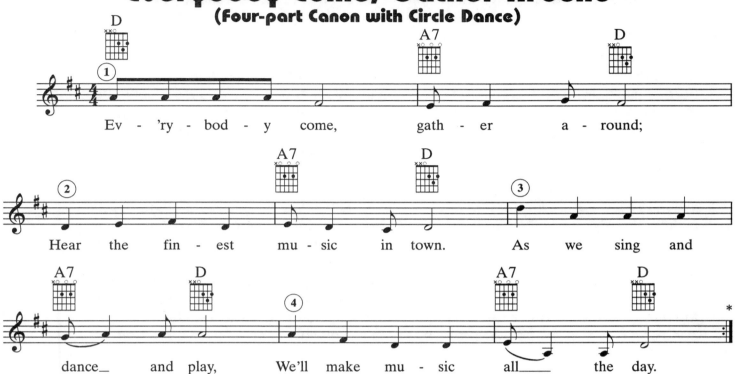

*This song is recorded first in unison, then in two, then three, then four parts.

The Circle Dance:

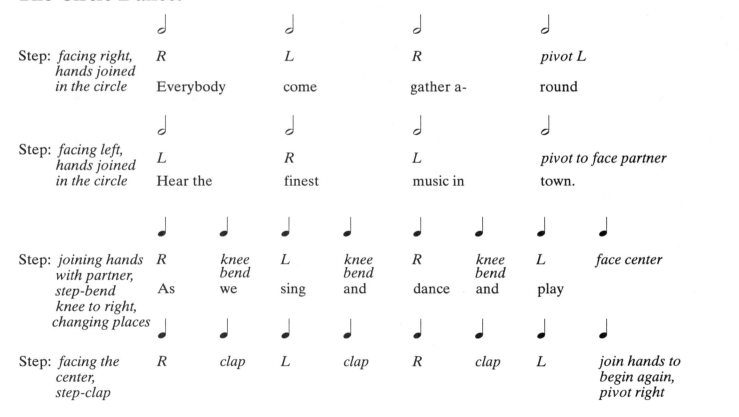

		R	L	R	pivot L
Step:	*facing right, hands joined in the circle*	Everybody	come	gather a-	round

		L	R	L	pivot to face partner
Step:	*facing left, hands joined in the circle*	Hear the	finest	music in	town.

		R	knee bend	L	knee bend	R	knee bend	L	face center
Step:	*joining hands with partner, step-bend knee to right, changing places*	As	we	sing	and	dance	and	play	

		R	clap	L	clap	R	clap	L	join hands to begin again, pivot right
Step:	*facing the center, step-clap*								

Everybody Come, Gather Around

⊙ Teaching Process:

1. This song is a four-part canon. First, perform the entire song for the class. Then teach the song by rote, in phrases. Have the children step the half-note macrobeat (♩) as you teach the song.

2. Divide the children into two, three, or four groups, depending on your assessment of their vocal independence in a canonic context. Assign the order of entrance into the canon and have the children sing the song in canon. Assist and refine as necessary.

3. Form a circle. Number the children by having them count off in 1's and 2's around the circle. Clarify the numbering by asking all of the 1's to raise their hands, and then ask the 2's to do the same. Explain that they are about to learn the circle dance that goes with the song and that they will need partners for the second part of the dance; 1's are to partner with the 2's to their right.

4. Teach the circle dance. The directions are below the music.

5. When the children know the circle dance, have them sing the song and perform the dance simultaneously. *Tip: Although this dance is very simple, it will be challenging for some students. Be prepared to observe varying levels of coordination and ability to combine singing and movement. Encourage the children to do their best.*

6. When they are comfortable in canon, have each small group form a circle and do the dance while singing their part in canon with the rest of the groups. The dance can be enhanced by the use of colored scarves gently tied around the wrists of the dancers. *Note: Perform the song and dance in canon with scarves to create a wonderful opening to a program.*

⊙ Assessment: *Musical Skill Achievement: Vocal Independence in a Canon*

What: Are the children able to remain vocally independent on their part while singing in canon?

How:

1. When the children know the canon well and are comfortable with the melody and have performed the song in canon as a group, inform them that you are going to listen to them sing the canon in small groups so that you may assess their ability to hold their part while they sing in canon. Explain that as you listen to them, you will give them a "+" (plus) if they remain independent and on their part and a "|" (half plus) if they do not remain independent. *Tip: A third level of achievement, "~," may be useful if you wish to indicate those who are wavering in their vocal independence.* To establish a sense of security in the children, you may want to first do this exercise just by telling them that you will be observing (without marking/grading) their performances and coaching them on ways to improve their part singing.

2. Divide the class into groups of four or eight.

3. Provide the class the opening pitch of the song, and play a D-major chord. Then, allow the class some time to practice in their groups. This should last no longer than five to ten minutes.

4. Ask for a volunteer group to start; otherwise, choose a group to start. As the groups sing, mark your data collection instrument according to your observations. *Tip: You may want to use the CD instrumental track to accompany the groups. Otherwise, you can play a simple chord accompaniment to keep them in the same key area. If you accompany the groups, you will need to recall your observations and write them down immediately following the performances.*

Assessment Framework:

Type: Formative, Structured Experience
Assessable Component: Musical Skill Achievement: Vocal Independence in a Canon
Assessment Response Mode: Performance
Tool: Observation
Materials: Data collection instrument, pen or pencil for marking
Scoring Guide: Bi- or multilevel, single criterion
Criterion: The student sings independently in a canon
Levels of Achievement: + = demonstrated; | = not demonstrated; if desired: ~ = wavers

Recommended Grade Level: 5

National Content Standard:
1—Singing, alone and with others, a varied repertoire of music

The Calypso Walk

I was walk-ing a - long__ to the ca - lyp - so beat, when

my old friend__ I came up - on; From my ca - lyp - so head__ to my ca -

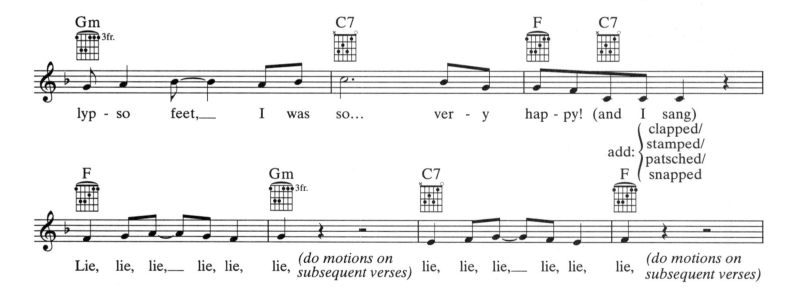

lyp - so feet,__ I was so... ver - y hap - py! (and I sang)

add: { clapped/ stamped/ patched/ snapped }

Lie, lie, lie,__ lie, lie, lie, *(do motions on subsequent verses)* lie, lie, lie,__ lie, lie, lie, *(do motions on subsequent verses)*

Lie, lie, lie,__ lie, lie, lie, lie,__ lie, lie, lie,__ lie, lie, lie. *(do motions on subsequent verses)*

This song is recorded five times to add clapping, stamping, patsching, and snapping on each repeat.

The Calypso Walk

Feel free to reproduce this page as needed. It may be enlarged or used as an overhead visual.

I was walking along to the calypso beat,

When my old friend I came upon;

From my calypso head to my calypso feet

I was so very happy
(and I sang

    clapped

      stamped

        patsched

          snapped):

Lie . . .

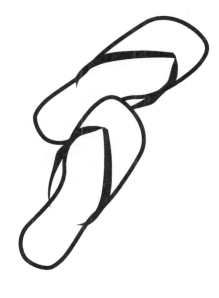

The Calypso Walk

☺ Teaching Process:

1. This is a cumulative song with movement. First, perform the song only for the class. Then, teach the song one phrase at a time. *Tip: It is helpful for older children to see the words of the song. A visual is provided for you on page 39. Because the words to the refrain are only "lie," a visual for the refrain is not necessary.*

2. When the children know the song, add the movement as follows:

            I   was   walking   along to   the   calypso   beat,
   Movement: *create a "calypso walk" of your own—rolling arms, stepping the beat, etc.*

        When my   old   friend I   came   upon;
   Movement: *wave to those around the room—all are friends!*

        From   my   calypso   head to   my   calypso   feet,
   Movement: *both hands touch head both hands touch feet*

        I   was   so   very happy (and I sang):
   Movement: *both hands wave upward on "so-o-o" and drop on "very happy"*

        Lie, lie (etc.)
   Movement: *during the refrain, the children create their own personal calypso walk, moving about the room*

3. Now it's time to add the accumulating verses. The verses add body percussion in the following order: clap, stamp, patsch, snap. *Tip: It is very helpful during this process to have small visuals for each phrase—"and I clapped," "and I stamped," "and I patsched," and "and I snapped"—or to point to the correct phrases using the visual on page 39.* Inform the children that you're now going to sing the song and add a new phrase, like this:

   I was walking along to the calypso beat, when my old friend I came upon;
   From my calypso head to my calypso feet, I was so-o-o very happy!
   And I sang, and I clapped…

       Lie, lie, lie, lie, lie, lie (♪♪♩, clapping)
       Lie, lie, lie, lie, lie, lie (♪♪♩, clapping)
       Lie, lie, lie, lie, lie, lie, lie, lie, lie, lie, lie, lie (♪♪♩, clapping).

   Be sure to perform the song with all of the movements, adding the phrase "and I clapped" at the end of the verse and clapping the ♪♪♩ pattern after phrases 1, 2, and 4 of the refrain.

4. Invite the children to sing the song again, adding the "and I clapped" phrase. *Tip: This is a good time to display the visual for this phrase.*

5. Add the next phrase, "and I stamped," so the end of the verse is now "and I sang, and I clapped, and I stamped…" *Tip: Display the visual for this phrase now.* To help the children know how this changes the refrain, sing the first phrase of the refrain as an example, adding the clapping and stamping as follows:

Lie, lie, lie, lie, lie, lie, ♪♪♩ (clapping) ♪♪♩ (stamping)

6. Have the children perform the song with both added body percussion phrases throughout the refrain.

7. Add the third phrase, "and I patched," so that the end of the verse is sung "and I sang, and I clapped, and I stamped, and I patched…" *Tip: Add the visual for this phrase at this time.* To help the children know how this changes the refrain, sing the first phrase of the refrain as an example, adding the clapping and stamping and patching, as follows:

Lie, lie, lie, lie, lie, lie, ♪♪♩ (clapping) ♪♪♩ (stamping) ♪♪♩ (patching)

8. Have the children perform the song with the three added body percussion phrases throughout the refrain.

9. Add the fourth phrase, "and I snapped," so that the end of the verse is sung "and I sang, and I clapped, and I stamped, and I patched, and I snapped…" *Tip: Add the visual for this phrase at this time.* To help the children know how this changes the refrain, sing the first phrase of the refrain as an example, adding the clapping, stamping, patching, and snapping as follows:

Lie, lie, lie, lie, lie, lie, ♪♪♩ (clapping) ♪♪♩ (stamping) ♪♪♩ (patching) ♪♪♩ (snapping)

10. Have the children perform the song with the four added body percussion phrases throughout the refrain.

11. Starting from the beginning, have the children perform the entire song, adding a new body percussion phrase each time. The song will need to be sung five times to complete the entire cycle.

Assessment: *Enabling Competency: Steady Beat* and *Creative Movement: Appropriateness of Movement*

What: Do the children demonstrate the steady beat and appropriate movement response during the performance of the song?

How:

1. Inform the children that you will be observing their performance of the song and dance to check for their ability to demonstrate the steady beat in a consistent manner and to create appropriate movement for the refrain. Explain that you will be marking their performance as follows: They will receive a "+" (plus) if they are demonstrating the beat consistently and a "|" (half plus) if they are not and that they will receive a "+" (plus) if their movements are appropriate, a "|" (half plus) if the movements are inappropriate, and a "0" if they are not creating any movements at all. *Tip: It is recommended that the children have a clear idea of what "appropriate movements" are so they know how to earn a "+". The best way to do this is to ask the children to demonstrate movements that are both appropriate and inappropriate for this song. Once they make a clear distinction between the two types of movements, explain that now they have shown you that they know the difference, so there is no reason for any of them to "accidentally" move in an inappropriate manner.*

2. As the children create movements and step to the beat, observe them closely for their demonstration of the steady beat and the appropriateness of their created movements. Mark your data collection instrument—grade book, seating chart, and so on—according to your observations.

☺ Assessment Framework:

Type: Formative, Structured Experience
Assessable Component: Enabling Competency: Steady Beat; Creative Movement: Appropriateness of Movement
Assessment Response Mode: Performance
Tool: Observation
Materials: Data collection instrument, pen or pencil for marking
Scoring Guide: Multilevel, multiple criterion
Criteria: The student demonstrates the steady beat
Levels of Achievement: + = demonstrated; | = not demonstrated
The student creates appropriate movements to the song
Levels of Achievement: + = demonstrated; | = not demonstrated; 0 = no movement response
Note: There will be two marks for every student during this assessment, such as: +/+; +/|, |/0, and so on.

Recommended Grade Level: 5

National Content Standard:
1—Singing, alone and with others, a varied repertoire of music

Friends in Music, Friends in Song
(Three-part Canon with Circle Dance)

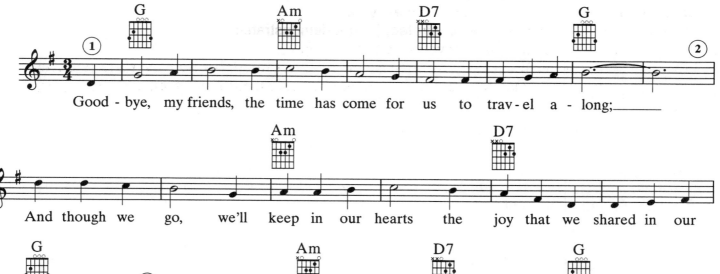

Good - bye, my friends, the time has come for us to trav-el a - long;

And though we go, we'll keep in our hearts the joy that we shared in our

song. Friends in mu - sic, friends in song.

*This song is recorded first in unison, then in two, then in three
parts with an 8-measure interlude inserted between repeats.

The Circle Dance:

Step: *facing right, hands joined in the circle*

R   L   R   L   R   L   R   *pivot center*

Goodbye, my friends, the time has come for us to travel along.

Step: *facing center, hands joined, raise hands slowly while stepping into the circle for four measures; lower them when reversing the step and returning to position*

R   L   R   L   R   L   R   *pivot left*

→ center ————————————→ circle

And though we go, we'll keep in our hearts the joy that we shared in our song.

Step: *facing left, hands joined in the circle*

L   R   L   R   L   R   L   *pivot right (to repeat)*

Friends   in   music,   friends   in   song.

Friends in Music, Friends in Song

Ⓔ Teaching Process:

1. This song is a three-part canon. First, perform the entire song for the class. Then, teach the song by rote, in phrases. Have the children step the dotted half-note macrobeat (♩.) as you teach the song.

2. Form a circle. Number the children by having them count off in 1's, 2's, and 3's around the circle. Clarify the numbering by asking all of the 1's to raise their hands, and then ask the 2's and 3's to do the same.

3. Divide the children into three groups, by the numbers they just counted off—all of the 1's will stand together, as will the 2's and the 3's. Assign the order of entrance into the canon and have the children sing the song in canon.

4. Bring them back together into one circle, and inform them that they are going to learn the circle dance for the song. Teach the circle dance. The directions are below.

5. When the children know the circle dance, have them sing the song and perform the dance simultaneously. *Tip: Although this dance is very simple, it will be challenging for some students. Be prepared to observe varying levels of coordination and ability to combine singing and movement. Encourage the children to do their best.*

6. When they are comfortable in canon, have each small group form a circle and do the dance while singing their part in canon with the rest of the groups. The dance can be enhanced by the use of colored scarves gently tied around the wrists of the dancers. *Note: Perform the song and dance in canon with scarves to create a wonderful opening to a program.*

Ⓔ Assessment: *Musical Skill Achievement: Singing in Canon*

What: Are the children able to remain vocally independent on their part while singing in canon?

How:

1. When the children know the canon well and are comfortable with the melody and have performed the song in canon as a group, inform them that you are going to listen to them sing the canon in small groups so that you may assess their ability to hold their part while they sing in canon. Explain that as you listen to them, you will give them a "+" (plus) if they remain independent and on their part and a "|" (half plus) if they do not remain independent. *Tip: A third level of achievement, "~," may be useful if you wish to indicate those who are wavering in their vocal independence.* To establish a sense of security in the children, you may want to first do this exercise just by telling them that you will be observing (without marking/grading) their performances and coaching them on ways to improve their part singing.

2. Divide the class into groups of three or six.

3. Provide the class the opening pitch of the song, and play a G-major chord. Then, allow the class some time to practice in their groups. This should last no longer than five to ten minutes.

4. Ask for a volunteer group to start; otherwise, choose a group to start. As the groups sing, mark your data collection instrument according to your observations. *Tip: You may want to use the CD instrumental track to accompany the groups. Otherwise, you can play a simple chord accompaniment to keep them in the same key area. If you accompany the groups, you will need to recall your observations and write them down immediately following the performances.*

Assessment Framework:

Type: Formative, Structured Experience
Assessable Component: Musical Skill Achievement: Vocal Independence in a Canon
Assessment Response Mode: Performance
Tool: Observation
Materials: Data collection instrument, pen or pencil for marking
Scoring Guide: Bi- or multilevel, single criterion
Criterion: The student sings independently in a canon
Levels of Achievement: + = demonstrated; | = not demonstrated; if desired: ~ = wavers

Teacher's Notes

Teacher's Notes

Your Source for Orff

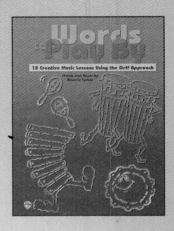

AN ACOUSTIC JAM (IN MIDDLE SCHOOL CLASS)
by Marilyn Copeland Davidson
(BMR08007)
This exceptional collection utilizes popular copyrights in an Orff instrument setting. There are opportunities for improvisation in every song, cambiata parts for boys' changing voices, and teaching suggestions that support the National Music Standards.

BROUGHT TO YOU BY... A COMMERCIAL REVUE
A Musical for Orff Ensembles by Bob de Frece and Sue Harvie
Teacher's Book with Reproducible Script and Visuals
(0587B)
Brought to You By... is a very funny musical revue accompanied by Orff instruments. It features 30 minutes of commercials that may be presented in their entirety or performed separately.

CONGA TOWN
by Jim Solomon
(BMR08002)
Percussion ensembles for upper elementary and middle school.

D.R.U.M.: DISCIPLINE, RESPECT, AND UNITY THROUGH MUSIC
by Jim Solomon
(BMR08009)
Kids love drums! This book is designed to stress teamwork and self-discipline while learning these intensive percussion ensembles built on music from the United States, Brazil, Africa, and China.

KIDS MAKE MUSIC SERIES: KIDS MAKE MUSIC, BABIES MAKE MUSIC, TOO!
by Lynn Kleiner with Cecilia Riddell
(BMR07002) Teacher's Book (Babies - Age 7)
(BMR07002CD) CD Only
More than 80 easy-to-follow, innovative lesson plans. Includes movement activities, instrument playing, puppets and more. Parent books with CDs available also for babies – age 8. Lynn Kleiner instrument kits and videos available from REMO, Inc.

IN ALL KINDS OF WEATHER, KIDS MAKE MUSIC!
by Lynn Kleiner
(BMR07007) Teacher's Book
(BMRCD07007) CD with All Songs from Teacher's Book
Enjoy 35 weather songs, poems, and stories that will delight children and stimulate their responses to music.

MI-RE-DO: THE GAME SHOW (WHO WANTS TO BE A MUSIC WIZ?)
A Musical for Orff Ensembles by Bob de Frece and Sue Harvie
Teacher's Book with Reproducible Script and Visuals
(BMR06005)
Joe (or Jane) Kid tries his luck on an exciting new game show in which he competes with the famous composers W.A. Mozart, J.S. Bach, and Carl Orff to answer questions about music. A reproducible student's script is included

MUSIC FOR FUN!
For Pre-K Through 2nd Grade Classes with Bob McGrath, "Bob on Sesame Street," and Marilyn Copeland Davidson
(BMR07009S) Student Book Only
(BMR07009CD) Teacher's Book and CD
A delightful music curriculum based on appealing songs recorded by "Bob on Sesame Street."

NAME GAMES (ACTIVITIES FOR RHYTHMIC DEVELOPMENT)
by Doug Goodkin
(BMR08008)
Doug has created a unique way to teach music by using "name games." A potpourri of games for all age levels includes Spelling Name • Name Stories • Icky Bicky Soda Cracker • Rumplestiltskin • Birthday Groups, and many more.

A RHYME IN TIME
by Doug Goodkin
(BMR08006)
Language, movement, and music activities for grades K–8 with open structures adaptable to the skill level of any group. Includes: One-Two, Tie My Shoe • Wee Willie Winkie • Bate Bate Chocolate • Tantos Rios • Second Story Window • Whoops! Johnny • Two Little Blackbirds, and many more.

SONGS OF LATIN AMERICA: FROM THE FIELD TO THE CLASSROOM (CANCIONES DE AMÉRICA LATINA: DE SUS ORÍGENES A LA ESCUELA)
by Patricia Shehan Campbell and Ana Lucía Frega
(0562B) Book and CD
Complete with native and conventional recordings of each piece! Also includes maps, cultural and musical information for each country, and lesson plans.

TRADITIONAL SONGS OF SINGING CULTURES: A WORLD SAMPLER
by Patricia Shehan Campbell, Sue Williamson, and Pierre Perron
(BMR05123CD) Book and CD
An Orff supplement with traditional folk tunes from all over the world.

WORDS TO PLAY BY
by Rhonda Tucker
(0543B)
Rhonda Tucker's poems are the basis for her very creative music lessons, which teach notation, forms, improvisation, ostinati, syncopation, bordurs, changing meters, and other musical concepts. In addition, she includes suggestions for starting a school Orff program.

YES, TODAY!...WE SING AND PLAY: ENCORE UNE FOIS!...AMUSONS NOUS
In English and French
by Ada Vermeulen
(BMR08012)
This book uses 15 songs, sound gestures, body percussion, instrument accompaniments, and movement games. Also includes great easy-to-follow diagrams for teaching games and dances.

MUSIC FOR CHILDREN (MURRAY EDITION)
This series by Carl Orff and Gunild Keetman is the English adaption of the German edition. Volume 1 contains speech and rhythmic exercises, nursery rhymes, songs using the major scale, and drone bass simple chords. Volume 3 contains increased instrumentation and range of keys. Volume 4 has songs using the Aeolian, Dorian, and Phrygian modes.
(ST04865) Volume 1, Pentatonic
(ST04866) Volume 2, Major: Drone Bass - Triads
(ST04867) Volume 3, Major: Dominant and Subdominant Triads
(ST04868) Volume 4, Minor: Drone Bass Triads
(ST10920) Volume 5, Minor: Dominant and Subdominant Triads
(ST12380CD) Volume 5, Accompanying CDs

DISCOVERING ORFF
(STAP099)
by Jane Frazee and Kent Kreuter
Designed for those who want detailed, practical assistance in the use of Orff techniques and materials in the classroom.

ELEMENTARIA
(ST11152)
by Gunild Keetman
A practical handbook to Orff-Schulwerk. Gives suggestions, examples, solutions, and practical guidance to teachers.

EXPLORING ORFF
(STAP076)
by Arvida Steen
Addresses critical questions about customizing programs to fit students' needs, selection of materials, and lesson plans.

MUSICA ACTIVA
(STAP054)
by Jos Wuytach
This book focuses on the element of rhythm based on the principles of Carl Orff.